GREEN VALLEY

W9-BYI-505

JUN - - 2005

Just the Opposite
Wet
Dry

Sharon Gordon

BENCHMARK BOOKS

MARSHALL CAVENDISH
NEW YORK

The park is wet.

The park is dry.

The swing is wet.

The swing is dry.

The slide is wet.

The slide is dry.

The bench is wet.

The bench is dry.

The table is wet.

The table is dry.

The sandbox is wet.

The sandbox is dry.

The sidewalk is wet.

The sidewalk is dry.

The playground is wet.

The playground is dry.

My class is wet.

So am I!

Words We Know

bench

class

park

playground

sandbox

20

sidewalk

slide

swing

table

Index

Page numbers in **boldface** are illustrations.

bench, **8**, 8–9, **9**, **20**

class, 18, **18**, **20**

dry, 3, **3**, 5, **5**, 7, **7**, 9, **9**, 11, **11**, 13, **13**, 15, **15**, 17, **17**

me, 19, **19**

park, **2**, 2–3, **3**, **20**
playground, **16**, 16–17, **17**, **20**

sandbox, **12**, 12–13, **13**, **20**
sidewalk, **14**, 14–15, **15**, **21**
slide, **6**, 6–7, **7**, **21**
swing, **4**, 4–5, **5**, **21**

table, **10**, 10–11, **11**, **21**

wet, 2, **2**, 4, **4**, 6, **6**, 8, **8**, 10, **10**, 12, **12**, 14, **14**, 16, **16**, 18, **18**, 19, **19**

About the Author

Sharon Gordon has written many books for young children. She has also worked as an editor. Sharon and her husband Bruce have three children, Douglas, Katie, and Laura, and one spoiled pooch, Samantha. They live in Midland Park, New Jersey.

With thanks to Nanci Vargus, Ed.D.
and Beth Walker Gambro, reading consultants

Benchmark Books
Marshall Cavendish
99 White Plains Road
Tarrytown, New York 10591-9001
www.marshallcavendish.com

Library of Congress Cataloging-in-Publication Data

Gordon, Sharon.
Wet dry / by Sharon Gordon.
p. cm. — (Bookworms: Just the opposite)
Includes index.
Summary: Depicts familiar scenes at a park and a school playground on a rainy day
and then on a sunny day to demonstrate the concept of wet and dry.
ISBN 0-7614-1572-6
1. Water—Juvenile literature. 2. Evaporation—Juvenile literature.
3. Polarity—Juvenile literature. 4. English language—Synonyms and
antonyms—Juvenile literature. [1. English language—Synonyms and
antonyms.] I. Title II. Series: Gordon, Sharon. Bookworms. Just the
opposite.

QC920.G67 2004
551.57'7—dc21
2003010080

Photo Research by Anne Burns Images

Cover Photos by Jay Mallin
All of the photographs used in this book were taken by and used with the permission of Jay Mallin.

Series design by Becky Terhune

Printed in China
1 3 5 6 4 2